D1477304

Mike Peyton is known through the yachting press of many countries for his special brand of cartoon and also for articles. Peyton fans have been lucky since many of his drawings were collected in book form in *Come Sailing* (1975) and *Come Sailing Again* (1976). He lives on an estuary in Essex, England. Much of his energy is devoted to seeing that the situations he depicts do not happen on board *Brimstone* and *Lodestone*, two ferro charter boats. He reckons he is reasonably successful in this as people keep coming back.

Mike Peyton

Hurricane Zoë and other Sailing

Nautical

Copyright © Michael Peyton 1977

Published in Great Britain 1977 by
NAUTICAL PUBLISHING CO LTD
Lymington, Hampshire SO4 9BA

All rights reserved, including the right
to reproduce this book, or parts thereof in any
form.

ISBN 0 245 53132 7

Filmset, printed and bound in
Great Britain by R. J. Acford Ltd.,
Chichester, Sussex

Caution!
Drawings . . .

After I had been sailing for about ten years
and my world had polarized into those that sailed
and those that did not, I realized that I had made
a mistake. Since then I have spent the past ten years
trying to prevent other people from making the
same mistake as myself, and getting themselves into
the sad and sorry situations I have done: situations
ranging from the relatively mild, such as almost
losing the entire family, to the traumatic ordeal of
losing one's ship. Plus the almost constant
arguments and altercations with wife, children,
bank manager, neighbors, harbor-masters and even,
occasionally, I must admit, other yachtsmen. It has
been an almost single-handed campaign carried
on in the best and only way I know, by cautionary
drawings, and backed solely by a few far-seeing
and public-spirited editors and my publisher. As
yet in Europe we have had little success, but I
welcome the opportunity to spread the campaign to
the States, whose people have so often given us the
lead in other fields. I am confident that they will
see these drawings in the spirit for which they were
designed.

Dedicated to Bob, Lynn and Melissa and other
members of the Sailing Club of the
Chesapeake, whose only fault was that they
were so well organized that they were useless
as cartoon material.

"Notice anything strange about the cloud formation Dave?"

"Ed Maylor Junior, Detroit."

*"On the box it said you would be surprised by the delicate
and intriguing flavor."*

"They shot the TV commercial for the island right here."

"As you say, madam, no harm done, but the tide is falling."

"The boat sinks underneath us and what do you grab, flares, food, water, fishing line . . . no! credit cards!"

"For the minute let's forget the 'Save the bay' campaign and concentrate on us."

"Sure we'll contact Nader, but what are we going to do now!"

*"My instinct tells me to get the hell outta here, even
if your instinct tells you to fill the ice chest."*

*"Could you contact the coastguard Dave, it's urgent.
We're nearly out of ice."*

"And when you get ashore, daddy will throw you a line."

"Hold your course Dave, we don't want to confuse him now!"

"We cannot stop, we're racing, but if you sail 270° for thirty two miles you should be OK."

"We won't argue now."

*"Where did I get the idea from? Well I was watching this
old movie with Jane Russell in it when, bingo!"*

"You should have kept your goddam 'Tin Star syndrome' cracks, until we were tied up to a dock."

"What do you think of her honey?"

"I feel sick, honey, sea sick."

26

"Can you imagine a foreign yacht getting a welcome like this back home?"

"Goddam motor boats!"

"Bad report on the radio Ed 'Data Teckniks' down five points."

"I can hear an engine – a lawn mower's."

"Before you turn in, left is port and port is red, correct?"

"Cal '36'. Alberg 30."

"Dear Captain Sankey: I took your correspondence course in seamanship and navigation and passed with honors . . . . ."

"Tell Ed it's clear, I can turn the shaft by hand."

"No I've no interest in boats, I'm in the loans
business. I just like to stroll around and look at
my floating assets."

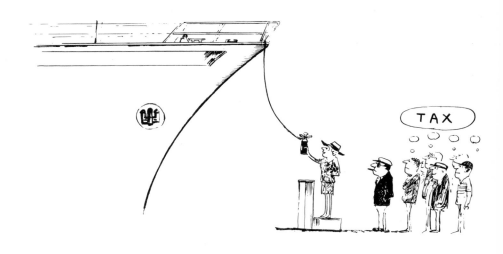

"I christen this ship 'Loop Hole'."

"She's plenty of power."

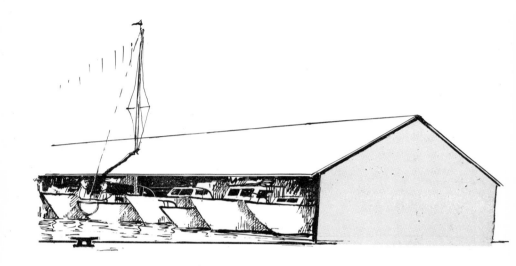

"*Of course there's enough goddam water here, I'm standing on my wheelhouse.*"

*"Don't worry. If we get it back I'll find a way of
marketing it."*

"Are you sure we're only 22 ft. overall?"

"We're not the only ones who think it beautiful. That sign
reads 'Site for Palm Island Marine Hotel complex,
twenty storeys . . . . .' "

"Civilization alright Bob, I can read the signs: Drugs, gas, eats, topless . . . . ."

"They sure must have had a rough trip."

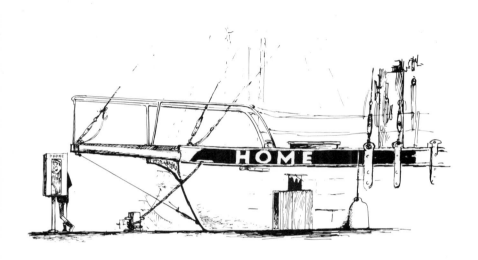

"I saw your commercial last night 'Phone for a loan for home improvements'."

"And to think it all started with a trial subscription to a sailboat magazine."

"That's not his wife."

"What does she cruise at?"

"Well – If they are waving, wave back."

*"Have you no soul. The boat's on a mooring, a hurricane
warning out and all you can think about is sex."*

"I assume if you know enough about tides to come close inshore to get out of it, you'll know it's rising."

*"You noticed it too: whenever the wind gets over 10 knots
your ears burn."*

"*You know you told me water on the left and gas on the right, well I turned round.*"

"The fixed white dead ahead, Dan."

"There are times when I miss the old rat race."

"He's out working on his boat."

"After all, Ed, it's over two months since we were here."

"Leave go and get up there, where's the Walter Mitty in you?"

"You're on, Bob."

"I sometimes think Dave's not the navigator he says he is."

"It reads 'Hello! My name is Cindy Diefenbaker'."

"Wouldn't be so bad if it was a hamburger and coffee, but that cost eighteen-fifty."

*"Never mind what it reminds you of; sort the goddam
thing out!"*

*"This is Bud Weiss your dock captain speaking. Welcome
alongside number nine dock, Dog Creek Marine. We
are floating at sea level, wind is 3 knots from the south
west, precipitation . . . . ."*

*"I tell you frankly you're my last resort. I've tried every-
thing else. It's this 'Swan 41' Identical boat to mine,
but it points higher and sails faster."*

"On a night like this it's a lifesaver."

"And I wish I was watching the midnight movie."

*"We're looking for a raft of seven boats dragging their
anchor. Have you seen them?"*

"Don't panic Bob just hand me my life preserver and the flares."

"Now just one more with you laid on your back as we found you."

"It must be one of those freak waves you read about."

"*After an evening like that, I'm glad I haven't got far to go.*"

"Hang on, we'll be back when we finish the race."

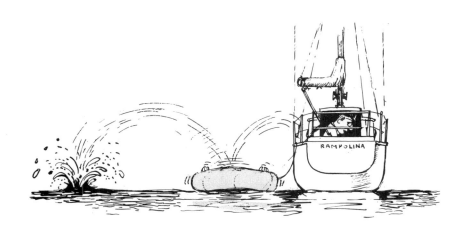

"Take it easy getting into that dinghy honey."

"Could you give me a bearing on Point Bonito?"

"And this is your Captain speaking!"

*"If we get back and they make a film of it I guess they'll
write another woman into it and make you black."*

"Schultz, I don't want any keen sailors working for this
outfit, they spend more time thinking about their boats
than their work. You're fired."

*"And, let me tell you, when he can tie a bowline and tell
port from starboard, we're out of a job."*

"*Best navigator I've had and never been wrong with weather forecasts or windshifts.*"

"Not on the chart!"

"D'you know my wife thinks we're stupid."

"It's nice to get in and relax."

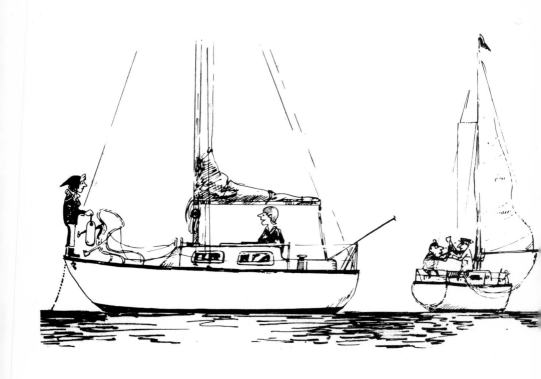

"I'm Nancy, come and have a coffee until they sort it out."

"Junior don't touch anythi . . . . ."